Words *for a* Mountain

Words for a Mountain

Words *for a* Mountain

Richard Kent

Foreword by Monica Wood

Credits

"The Little Pass Holder" © Jill Bartash

"Katie Collette Racing" © John Bernard (RiverValleyGraphics.com)

"Julie Parisien Pond Skimming" and Author Photo © Kate Clough (KateCloughPhotographs.com)

"After the Storm" and "Aurele Legere Ski Jump" © Richard Kent

"Greg Poirier Ski Jumping" © John Leckey

"A Brief History of Skiing in the River Valley" was originally written in 2004 for the Nordic Museum in the new lodge at Black Mountain. The museum committee– Paul Jones, Joe Sassi, Herb Adams, Muriel Arsenault, Chummy Broomhall, and Richard Kent–gathered this material from the Chisholm Ski Club archives, Ski Museum of Maine, and personal files.

"Summer Jump" first appeared in *Maine Life* © 1979 Richard Kent

"Skiing Indy" © 1978 Mike Moxley, first appeared in the *Indianapolis Star Magazine*.

Writing Athletes LLC
WritingAthletes.com
Copyright © 2013 Richard Kent
All rights reserved.
ISBN-10: 0986019143
ISBN-13: 978-0-9860191-4-2

For little ski areas everywhere.

Profits from the sale of this book
go to support Black Mountain.

"We're a small mountain, but we do big things."

Chummy Broomhall
"We're in this Together"
Powder Magazine, July 25, 2013

Contents

FOREWORD

One winter day when I was in eighth grade, Sister Mary Ella unlocked her supply cupboard and unearthed a gray bucket filled with crayons. We were thirteen years old—practically grownups!—but here was our strict, exacting teacher waving fistfuls of Crayolas and encouraging us to—how can I say it?—*have fun*. A snow scene would be nice, she suggested; something festive and frolicky. She allowed us to leave our seats without permission, to look at one another's work, to move our desks from their pre-appointed positions. She'd recently reclaimed her baptismal name, from lumpen "Sister Mary Ernest" to airy "Sister Mary Ella" overnight. Perhaps this reclamation had rattled loose a long-lost spark of whimsy, the "la-la-la" of her true name at last bursting into song.

We selected our crayons, suspiciously at first; it could be a trick. I started with Midnight Blue, Bittersweet, and Pine Green. There was a big run on White. Some of us drew children cavorting in suburban yards between snow-trimmed boxwoods and picture windows, a Dick-and-Jane idyll that didn't much exist in the real life of our town. The rest of us drew scenes we knew firsthand: kids skating on a flooded ball field, a plume of mill smoke rising across the river; kids sardined onto toboggans at the top of Harlow Hill; and kids—lots and lots of kids—skiing down the iconic slope of Black Mountain.

I was not a skier. I knew the mountain not as a winter wonderland but rather as part of the ring of hills that enclosed our valley year-round. To me, Black Mountain was merely a distant blaze of light in autumn, or a springtime waft of fragile, promising greens. But if you lived in its lovely shadow, that mountain made itself known whether you skied it or not. And so, after Sister Ella's bewildering request, I made a picture of a genderless figure slaloming down the mountain, its knees headed east, heels headed west, skis on the angle, poles close to the body and rushing back.

Timmy Gallant wandered over from the boys' side of the room and admired my imagined ski slope, which by this time I'd populated with a dozen skiers in ballooning parkas colored in Periwinkle and Violet Blue. "I've never seen you at the mountain," he said.

"I don't ski."

He frowned over my page, pointing to one of the figures. "Then how did you draw that?" He meant the skier's form, the poles, the skis, the boots, the boot buckles, the everything.

"I don't know." I really didn't.

"You must have skied at least once," he said. "Right?" He looked deliciously doubtful. A shudder of pride went through me, for I had a crush on Timmy and he was at this moment recognizing that I was the greatest artist in the world.

"I don't believe you," he said.

At this I took offense. True, I had never skied, but like Sister Ella fulfilling the cheerful possibilities of her given name, I'd tapped into something I didn't know I remembered. Had weekly photos of bright-cheeked racers in the *Rumford Falls Times* stayed in my head without my noticing? Or maybe I'd heard enough ski stories from Bunny Fournier, my first friend, to imagine that I'd sped down that mountain myself, holding my poles just so, bracing against the spray of snow while bearing right, bearing left, whoosh-whoosh.

I did, finally, convince Timmy that I'd never been on the mountain in winter. But I knew enough then, and I know enough now, to understand what this mountain means to all of us who still love our River Valley hometowns. To each of us, the words "Black Mountain" conjure sudden, bright images unique to us: two feet of perfect powder on Christmas Eve; a lone hiker and his dog silhouetted against a waning sun; a six-point buck flitting into a copse of fall-red trees. For me, it's my sister's July wedding at the lodge, a day so happy I thought the mountain itself might levitate with joy.

But mountains don't move much, and this one will exist long after our last grandchildren beget their last grandchildren. When we say we want to save Black Mountain, we mean our roots, our family stories, our sense of place. Silent witness to enormous change—bad economy, foreign competition, lost jobs—this mountain will endure as long as the earth from which it rises, its lordly presence absorbing our collective memory. *I don't need saving*, it seems to tell us. *But perhaps I might save you.*

Monica Wood
Portland, Maine

ACKNOWLEDGEMENTS

Books, like small-town ski areas, are community affairs. My writing community for this project included Katie Dunn, a long-time skier, whose enthusiastic feedback to an early draft inspired my writing. Gayle Sirois has always been an advocate—her words and advice as my primary reader played an important role in this book project and in others. For over 30 years, Anne Wood has been my editor. No writer could have a more important wordsmith in his corner—no person could have a more treasured friend.

When I asked Monica Wood if she'd write a foreword to this book, she said, in effect, "In a heartbeat." Thanks, Monnie! Her new book, *When We Were the Kennedys: A Memoir from Mexico, Maine*, shines a dazzling light on our community.

John Bernard (*River Valley Graphics*), Kate Clough (*Kate Clough Photographs*), and Jill Bartash generously donated photographs and their time. Many other photographs from days gone by have been included in this book—thank you to those anonymous photographers for capturing a bit of our history.

The research for "A Brief History of Skiing in the River Valley" was a team effort and came from the legwork of Black Mountain's 2004 Museum Committee: my new friend Paul Jones, my high school ski coach Herb Adams, and my dear friend the late Joe Sassi.

My thanks to Roger Arsenault for his enthusiastic support of this project and for his tireless work on behalf of Black Mountain.

I am indebted to Paul Jones, the Chisholm Ski Club's historian and curator. Paul's love of history and River Valley skiing shines through as he researches, writes about, and cares for our community's skiing legacy.

Finally, and not least, Andy Shepard, Maine Winter Sports Center, and the Libra Foundation helped transform our mountain. Their contributions of time, expertise, and funding are a profound gift, and legacy, to the River Valley community. We owe them our thanks, and a promise, to continue on as thoughtful stewards of Black Mountain.

INTRODUCTION

Like many families in the River Valley, ours *lived* at Black Mountain during the winter months. The five Kent kids skied through Saturday morning lessons, onto the Chisholm Junior Ski Team, and up to the high school team. For us, winter meant "the mountain"—it still does for many in our community and beyond.

Nowadays, when driving up to the mountain to ski, run, or hike, I recall what was perhaps the perfect winter's day at Black Mountain for a young skier in the 1960s. The Fire Station's horn sounds and WRUM 790 confirms it: No School! We slap bologna and cheese on white bread, wrap the sandwiches in waxed paper, and stuff them into our parka pockets. Our ski equipment is loaded into our hulking International Travelall, a precursor to today's SUVs. Then, as always, our mother's ski-day refrain: "Skis, boots, poles? Clean underwear?" By 1971, we had shattered three legs and two arms, and in my mother's eyes, woe unto the child who ends up in Rumford Hospital with unsightly underwear.

We plow through the bank of snow at the bottom of our driveway. Falls Hill has been sanded, but the hard-packed snow repels the sand. No matter. Our mother knows winter driving. All the way down she applies the brakes with rhythmic precision—press and release, press and release. At the foot of the hill, we turn left onto Spruce Street and drive past the row of apartment buildings where papermakers like my father have settled in for a restless day of sleep after the night shift.

Two turns past Breau's Dairy and we approach the big hills. My mother guns it. Go, Ma! Go! We fishtail and cheer our way past smaller cars that have failed the climb. Some of those drivers will try again; others will head back to town for a hot breakfast. But in our behemoth, we crest the first hill with speed to spare. After the short decline we shoot up the second hill, skid around the hard right turn at the top, and settle onto the flats of Isthmus Road. It's all downhill from here.

In the lodge we meet up with friends whose parents own heavy cars like ours. High-pitched voices ricochet off the paneled walls of the lodge. Wasting no time, we zip up our parka collars to our chins, position and reposition our goggles. Once outside, long-thong straps wrapped and tugged tight, we study the hefty quilt of fresh powder and call out the trails we want to hit first. "Expert!" "Night!" "Let's tuck the Woods!"

Wading through the deep snow in an awkward skate, we reach the T-bar. The lift operator nods to us; he's a reliable high school kid who owns a car and soon will be drafted to Vietnam. Dressed in a greasy one-piece work suit, he guides the red bar toward our hands. We twist it slightly and scooch for the wood. There's a moment of stillness—a clank—then that lurch. We glide off into swirling snow with the first tower's clinkety-clinkety-clank above us. And just like that, Black Mountain is ours for the day.

This is the way it has always been at the mountain, kids and families, lollipop races and potluck suppers. On Friday nights, friends wedge into the Last Run Lounge and on Saturdays, you'll see the Chisholm Ski Club's *Red Army* supporting cross-country skiers from Maine to Alaska as they gear up to challenge High School Hill. And yes, just like 50 years ago, there's the blessed snow day and the clinkety-clinkety-clank of the new lifts carrying Black Mountain's next generation up into winter's enchantment.

"Where We Are From"

I am not a poet by trade, but the western mountains of Maine, our openhearted communities, and the mountain's legacy of family, friends, and recreation do bring out such language. When we learned of the struggles Black Mountain faced—the possibility of its closing—many of us shared our stories on social media and in person. Hearing those stories got me thinking, and as writers have done through the ages, I opened my notebook and put pencil to paper.

For some readers—especially the younger ones—this poem, modeled after "Where I'm From" by George Ella Lyon, includes some unfamiliar language from the past. "Pine tar? Bear traps? What's a long-thong?" You could *Google* these terms—but better yet, why not ask your great-aunt or your grandpa next time you're on the ski slopes or hanging out at the lodge. Their words, their stories, will enrich this one, making *Words for a Mountain* a family affair… just like our mountain.

Where We Are From

Allen Kent, Scotty's Mountain, 1957

WHERE WE ARE FROM

We are from long-thong straps
and Look-Nevada combinations.
We are from wooden Kneissls, plastic K2's, and the
cold black steel of Head Competitions
that carried us down the slopes of Black Mountain.

Ski racer from the 1960's

We are from boot-top fractures and hand-held timing,
from lace-up leather boots and bamboo slalom gates;
we know flag starts, pine tar, and the blow torch... and
we still rear back on our toes when we hear "Racer ready!"

THE NEW CHISHOLM

SKI PARK

A VIEW OF THE PROPOSED SKI AREA

Located at

BLACK MOUNTAIN

Rumford, Maine

"The Only Complete Ski Area in the East"

Chisholm Ski Club Corporation
Common Stock Informational Brochure, c. 1959

We are from the opening day at Black Mountain:
the 4th tower party, red hotdogs on a bonfire, hot chocolate,
and hay bales piled near the sleek new T-bar
that carried us toward the sky.

Charles "Slim" Broomhall, Coach Henderson, Wendall "Chummy" Broomhall
Spruce Street Tow, c.1940

We are from Christensen, Sorenson, and Mac MacFawn;
from P-Tex and paraffin, Northlands and Lunds.
We are Peterboroughs and the Paris ski made just up the road;
we wore bear traps and safety straps, ski brakes and Cubcos.

Scotty's Mountain Rope Tow, 1954

We are from Scotty's Mountain and
Liberty's slope in our backyard.
We jumped the graveyard hill on Sunnyside
and tucked the Night Trail at Chisholm Winter Ski Park.

Katie Collette "Shooting the Headwall on the Lower Androscoggin," 2013

We are from Cera Nova and Rode Extra Red,
from fall lines, flex poles, and freerides;
we freestyle and classic, Herringbone and V-2;
we are DNS, DNF, and "Walk back up or you D-S-Q."

Second Annual
Winter Carnival

The Chisholm Ski Club is about to hold its second Winter Carnival. The first was very successful but the Carnival officers profiting by their experiences of last year are planning a much more interesting carnival for this year.

The Ideal of the Club is that every child shall be taught to love to play in the great outdoors and to enjoy the fruits of health giving recreation in the crisp clear air and sunshine of the good old State of Maine.

February 9-10, 1925

We are from the *Red Army* and
Chisholm Junior Ski Team tag days,
from bake sales and potlucks,
ski swaps, raffles, and "Hit the track for Black."

Upper Slopes at Spruce Street Tow, late 1920's early 1930's

We are from a family of sibling slopes…
Titcomb, Saddleback,
Sugarloaf, and The River.
We raced Big Rock, Spruce,
Lost Valley, and Shawnee; and on a Tuesday
in late February, we skipped school to ski Mt. Abram's
with our mother.

Cross-Country Trail Signs, Black Mountain, 2013

We ate lunch in Muriel's Kitchen
and raced the trails of Squaw Valley;
we ran Russian Hill in Lake Placid, and
defended freedom with the 10th Mountain Division.

Chisholm Ski Club Jump, (a.k.a., The Suicide), Scotty's Mountain, 1954

We are from The Suicide and Aurele Legere ski jumps,
from High School Hill and the Lower Quirion Loop;
we rip the Terrain Park for backside air and
ride the rails living with TFR.

Swedish Skier, 1950 World Championships, Rumford, Maine
February 1-6, 1950

We raced the Telstar Schuss and the Wes Marco,
the Saddleback Cup and Mel Jodrey;
we are Mr. Roderick's Marathon-Tour and *The Broomhall Cup*,
the '50 World Championships and the NCAAs.
We are Pintos, Panthers, Falcons, and Hawks.

Joe West, Mountain Manager, c. 1962

We are from Saturday morning lessons
and the Last Run Lounge;
we are Joe West and Jim Carter,
Big Jeff and Houlie.

Spruce Street Tow, 1938

We cruised the Woods Trail and the Gully,
Upper Sunday and Magalloway—
we have skied Roger's Loop and Ray's 5k,
schussed the Spruce Street Tow back in the day.

Stephens High School Ski Team
State of Maine & New England High School Champions, 1964

We are from Mack Miller and Herbie Adams;
we bought K-2 Comps from Blackie's,
goggles and stretch pants from Hamann's;
we rode rope tows and pomas, chairlifts and T-bars.

U.S. Olympian and World Champion Julie Parisien, Pond Skimming, 2012

We are from winter carnivals and pond skimming,
from the Grenoble Olympics and
   "Here's little Jimmy Miller from Mexico, Maine"
   on *ABC's Wide World of Sports.*
We are skimeisters, specialists, lodge rats, and *shredders.*

"After the Storm in the River Valley Mountains"

We are from the shores
of the Swift, Ellis, and Androscoggin,
from the pine-laced feet of Glass Face, Whitecap, and Zircon
where our parents fit pipe, tested pulp, and breathed sulfur
to make paper to pay for our skis.

We are from expert trails and community,
from real snow days and hissing radiators
lined with mittens.

"The Little Passholder" —Jack Bartash, 2013

We are from Maine,
these western mountains,
our Black Mountain,
this River Valley–
home.

A Brief History of Skiing
in The River Valley

–Parts of this section were researched and written with
Herb Adams, Muriel Arsenault, Chummy Broomhall, Paul Jones, and Joe Sassi.–

Upper Slopes, Spruce Street Tow, c. 1930

Scandinavian papermakers introduced skiing to the River Valley in the late 1800's. In the early 20th century, before the chairlifts and multi-storied lodges, before snowmaking, snack bars, and rental shops, folks in the River Valley took to their neighborhood ski runs. These homegrown facilities with names such as "The Fields at French's Farm" served as the foundation for the community's love affair with skiing.

During this era, families formed outing clubs, skiing daredevils constructed jumps on hillsides, and ski tourists packed trails through thick pine forests and across the open fields along the Swift and Androscoggin Rivers. In time, the Spruce Street/Swain Road area surfaced as the central location for winter carnivals—it was here that the neighborhood skiers gathered to show their stuff.

In 1926, jumping enthusiasts constructed a 60-meter ski jump with a 190-foot tower at Spruce Street. A toboggan chute, skating rink, and 18-kilometer cross-country trail also appeared. In back of the Breau Farm on Swain Road, alpine skiers enjoyed the open hilly fields. There, slalom and wild downhill courses challenged young and old alike. In 1938, the Spruce Street ski facilities grew to include a tow bar lift—the slopes were also lit for night skiing.

In 1945, the Chisholm Ski and Outing Club built an all-natural jump on Scotty Richardson's property behind today's Mountain Valley High School. That ski area expanded over time, and by 1951 the lights from the Swain Road slopes were moved to Scotty's. In 1953, volunteers installed a 600-foot rope tow; the next year, an additional 650 feet of towline provided a unique dogleg to accommodate the varying terrain.

In 1960, the Chisholm Ski Club incorporated and purchased 450 acres of land at Glover farm on Black Mountain. The Chisholm Winter Ski Park would include a 2200-foot T-bar lift, a three-level lodge, three main slopes, night skiing, cross-country trails, and ski jumps. Since its opening day on February 19, 1961, the ski area at Black Mountain has undergone several name changes and ownership agreements. New lifts, trails, and a lodge as well as other 21st century ski-area amenities now grace the property—what hasn't changed is the spirit of community and the love affair with skiing that has, for over a century, permeated the River Valley.

Wendall "Chummy" Broomhall

Ski Jumping in the River Valley

In the 1920's, Norwegian Mat Nielsen is said to have built the first snow jumps out near the shooting range on Swain Road. Back then, ski jumpers flew a mere 30 to 40 feet off these natural jumps. Soon afterwards, with interest rising, a larger jump was constructed behind the old Israelson's Garage on Spruce Street and jumpers began flying up to 100 feet.

During the mid to late 1920's, Chisholm Ski Club members constructed one of the most modern and largest ski jumps in America at the Spruce Street site. After renovations in the 1930's, Aurele Legere of Rumford and two out-of-state jumpers shared the hill record of 185 feet. During the World War II years, the Spruce Street jump fell into disrepair and collapsed.

In 1946, the Ski Club held a jumping competition on an all-natural jump at Scotty's Mountain behind what is now Mountain Valley High School. Interest in ski jumping grew and soon, under the supervision of engineer Reidar Christiansen, a steel tower was erected at Scotty's. On February 10, 1957, Art Tokle of New Jersey's Telemark Ski Club set a hill record of 202 feet, and one year later International Ski Federation (FIS) team member Jim House of Iron Mountain, Michigan, set the new hill record of 211 feet.

Chisholm Ski Club Jump (a.k.a., The Suicide), c. 1954

In the late 1950's, a property dispute forced a move from Scotty's to Black Mountain. Ski Club members built three jumps for the various levels of competition. When Bates College landed the 1976 NCAA Ski Championships and chose to host the Nordic events at Black Mountain, upgrades to the ski jumps and cross-country trails began. During the NCAA Ski Jumping Championships, a record of 195 feet was set for the 55-meter hill.

Greg Poirier on the Aurele Legere Jump, 1976

In the early 1980's, US colleges dropped ski jumping from the NCAA championships and high schools in Maine and throughout the country soon followed. In the 1990's the Chisholm Ski Club maintained five ski jumps at Black Mountain of Maine but the sport failed to capture the imaginations of young skiing athletes. In December of 1999, the last ski jump in the River Valley was torn down, ending nearly eight decades of this spectacular sport.

In 1979, as Rumford High School's last ski jumping coach, I wrote the following poem in tribute to Aurele Legere and my fellow ski flyers:

SUMMER JUMP
In memory of Aurele Legere

It rests through the
Warmer months,
Graying in the sun.
The weathered boards
Creak as the towering monster
Sways in the summer wind.
Beneath the table a lost cake of
Paraffin melts,
The discarded flag that sent
So many into flight
Fades, and
Echoes can be seen when
Standing in the judges' box.
Through the fields below walks
A lonely flyer, tired of
Summer life.
Climbing to the top,
He reaches last winter
And dreams of the next.

In the woods behind my Prospect Avenue home, an abandoned ski jump sits at the base of a steep hill. Those days of backyard jumping with my brother Rob and our neighborhood friends prompted this haiku:

BACKYARD SKI JUMPERS

The backyard jump calls:
we dream daylong of Innsbruck
out over our skis.

The Aurele Legere Ski Jump, c. 1981

1950 FIS World Nordic Championships

In 1950, Rumford stepped onto the world ski racing stage.

Lake Placid was scheduled to play host to the International Ski Federation (FIS) World Nordic Championships. These competitions would be the first-ever in America and the first since the 1939 pre-war competitions in Zakopane, Poland. With bare ground in the New York skiing village, volunteers prepared the 65-meter jumping hill with 300 tons of crushed ice. However, as for the 18- and 50-kilometer cross-country ski trails, a timely snowfall remained the only solution to staging a race.

FIS officials explored numerous options for pulling off these cross-country competitions. After conferring with Rumford's Wendall "Chummy" Broomhall, FIS representatives dispatched two scouts some 300 miles east to tour the 18-kilometer Rumford trail. With the FIS scouts' enthusiastic endorsement, the Chisholm Ski and Outing Club and the entire River Valley community began preparing to host the Nordic skiing world.

Ironically, the move to the Rumford venue paused momentarily when Lake Placid received a five-inch snowstorm. The Swedish team rebelled against the organizing committee's indecision and headed east to Rumford, citing the lack of an adequate snow base in New York. Rumford's organizing committee served up its own ultimatum: Bring all of the cross-country races to Maine or find another site. The Rumford race was on.

Within two days nearly 100 competitors and 400 support staff arrived in Rumford to the kind of welcome for which the River Valley has become known. Hotels, guesthouses, and private homes opened their doors to the international contingent. Scores of Chisholm Ski and Outing Club members as well as volunteers from across Maine and New Hampshire worked to ready the trails. Beyond trail preparation, volunteers staffed committees for such needs as entertainment, plowing, parking, policing, and skier transportation.

On Friday, February 3, 1950, 70 competitors raced the first event, the 18-kilometer individual cross-country. Exhibition jumping took place on Saturday the 4th at Scotty's Mountain; on Sunday, the 40-kilometer military relay race started in front of an estimated crowd of 1500 spectators. Monday's 50-kilometer marathon began at 10 a.m. and later that afternoon the awards for the World Championships were presented in Rumford's Municipal Hall.

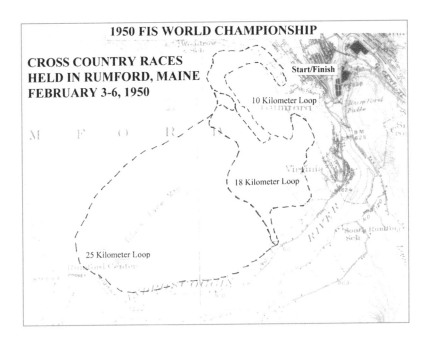

1950 FIS WORLD CHAMPIONSHIP

**CROSS COUNTRY RACES
HELD IN RUMFORD, MAINE
FEBRUARY 3-6, 1950**

Start/Finish

10 Kilometer Loop

18 Kilometer Loop

25 Kilometer Loop

Writing a "Where I'm From" Poem

WRITING YOUR OWN "WHERE I'M FROM" POEM

When we write about what we know and where we live, our writing rings true. This section of *Words for a Mountain* invites you to write your own "Where I'm From" poem. And once you're finished, why not post your piece on Black Mountain's Facebook page. Here's what I did to write mine.

I started by making lists from my own memory. I identified the people, places, and things of my skiing experiences. For example, I listed the names of my ski instructors like Mickey Arsenault; I remembered the equipment I used over the years like my Head Competitions and flashy K2 Comps; I named my coaches like Herb Adams, Chummy Broomhall, Tom Grace, and Chendy Chenard; I listed ski buddies like Greg Waite (the two of us were on the Chisholm Junior Ski Team together and years later coached the high school teams); I remembered mountain friends like Sue & Jeff Knight. With each name, stories emerged.

Next, because pictures spark memories, I paged through our family scrapbooks, reviewed a slew of photos, surfed different websites, and looked over newspaper clippings from my coaching days. One afternoon, I sat with Paul Jones in Patty's and his Dixfield living room and went through the Chisholm Ski Club's archive. I went up to the mountain and wandered through the lodge taking photographs. Whenever new words, stories, or ideas surfaced, I jotted them down in my notebook. I had a long list.

When it came to my poem, I tried as best as I could to make it universal and not about my family or my own experiences. That's why I used the pronoun "we" throughout. However, your poem should be a reflection of your family, friends, and personal experiences. Here's what you can do to gather ideas for your "Where I'm From" poem.

Grab a pencil and write in the space provided on the next few pages. For example, under "ski friends," just make a list of names. Or under "ski clothes," list a favorite parka or helmet. To make this poem more vivid to your readers, add colors, emotions, and other descriptions such as your "chatty friend Chester" or "favorite powder-blue parka." You can create these lists with your ski friends or family members. You might write this poem with another person. Simply put, there aren't any rules. And listen, please don't get all bound up trying to be perfect while you're writing these lists. Just put words on paper as soon as they pop into your head. As I used to say to my ski racers, "This ain't the Olympics. Have some fun!"

Worksheet for Writing a "Where I'm From" Poem

Ski friends: Trail names:

Lessons: Ski clothing:

Ski equipment: Favorite Expressions:

Foods   Ski instructors:

Races:

Ski activities
(e.g., pond skimming)

Perfect ski day:

Worst ski day:

Ski trips:

Other ski areas:

Other thoughts:

Stories: Make a list of your favorite ski stories. Don't write out the whole story, just summarize. For example, here's one of mine: The day my oldest brother Allen brought my brother Rob and me to the 20-meter jump for our first jump. I remember screaming "Ma!" as I went off.

Story:

Story:

Story:

Story:

Story:

Story:

Story:

Story:

Story:

<u>Photographs</u>: Gather some favorites. If you don't have your own collection, surf the websites of Black Mountain, the Chisholm Ski Club, or friends' Facebook pages. If you're from *away* and writing about your hometown ski area, check out your mountain's website. As you look through the photos, jot down what comes to mind.

Photo thoughts:

Finally, it's time to write a draft of the poem. Relax. Take a deep breath. This is not the Olympics. In my writing classes, I always provide the following Jacque Barzun quotation to my students:

> "To know how to begin to write is a great art. Convince yourself that you are working in clay, not marble; on paper, not eternal bronze; let the first sentence be as stupid as it wishes. No one will rush out and print it as it stands. Just put it down; and then another. Your whole first paragraph or first page may have to be guillotined after your piece is finished; but there can be no second paragraph until you have a first."

On the next page you'll see that I provided a prompt for the first stanza and enough space on the next two pages for your first draft. If you struggle with ideas, look back at my poem. You can also search online for "Where I'm From" poems and read a few more examples. I searched and landed 49,400,000 results. Don't read them all. Do read George Ella Lyon's original version. It's a gift.

WHERE I'M FROM

by _____

I am from _____ (e.g., a place on the mountain)

and _____ (e.g., a ski instructor's advice).

I am from _____ (e.g., an article of clothing)

and _____ (e.g., a mountain activity).

Congratulations, poet! Remember: If you'd like, share your poem on Black Mountain's Facebook page.

River Valley Skiing Historical Trivia

RIVER VALLEY SKIING HISTORICAL TRIVIA
(Answers may be found on page 74.)

1. List the Winter Olympians from the River Valley.

2. What was the official name of Black Mountain when it opened on February 19, 1961?

3. What was the price of an adult lift ticket when the mountain celebrated its Grand Opening on March 3-4, 1962?

4. In the early days of Black Mountain, what did skiers call the trail to the left of the T-bar?

5. In the early days of Black Mountain, what did skiers call the trail to the right of the T-bar?

6. Name the two ski shops in Rumford in the 1960s.

7. How did the Winter Carnival Queen get selected for the Chisholm Winter Carnival?

8. What was the price of a family season pass when the mountain celebrated its Grand Opening on March 3-4, 1962?

9. Who was Ron Houle?

10. Which mountain manager raced in the 1980 World Heavy Weight Ski Championships at Sugarloaf USA?

11. What is the River Valley's connection to the 1960 Olympics in Squaw Valley, California?

12. In the 1980's what non-skiing ski coach recruited hundreds of elementary and middle school students onto the Chisholm Junior Ski Team and built a championship program?

13. Name the 1964 championship ski racers and coach on page 44.

14. Who were the president, vice president, clerk, and treasurer of the Chisholm Ski Club Corporation that launched the purchase of Black Mountain in the late 1950's?

15. In what year was the first Chisholm Winter Carnival held?

Do you have a piece of history to share?

If you have questions you'd like to share to help unearth and preserve more of our local skiing history, please post them on Black Mountain's Facebook page for all to enjoy and consider.

1.

2.

3.

4.

5.

Answers to Trivia Questions

1. Chummy Broomhall, Robert Pidacks, Jack Lufkin, Frank Lutick, Jr., Jim Miller

2. Chisholm Winter Park

3. $3.00

4. The Night Trail

5. The Expert Trail

6. Blackie's and Hamann's

7. Whoever sold the most Carnival Tickets.

8. $75

9. Named mountain manager in December 1974.

10. Jeff Knight

11. Chummy Broomhall designed the cross-country course for this Winter Olympic trail.

12. Bill Morgan

13. *Top row:* Buddy Fisher, Gary Giberson, Coach Mack Miller, Avery Caldwell, Fred Kent, Larry Gillis; *Bottom row:* Pinky Cunningham, Greg Stewart, Lee Buotte, Mike Mickeriz

14. Benjamin J. Bernard, President; Richard Giberson, Vice President; Joseph Richard, Clerk; F. Melvin Aylward, Treasurer.

15. 1921

1959 – 2013

THE OXFORD LOG   November, 1959

Chisholm Ski Club Gets New Location

Members of the Chisholm Ski Club have acquired a new location for the development of a skiing area for the community. The new site is a 450-acre tract on Black Mountain near the Isthmus Road about four miles from the center of town and one-and-a-half miles beyond the Catholic Cemetery. The necessity of moving to this location was caused by the expiration of the lease at Scotties Mountain where the existing ski slope is located.

The above photograph shows the 2,300 foot mountain and the center section is where the 2,200 foot long intermediate ski slope and ski tow will be located. There will also be a beginners slope 600 feet long with a 65 meter jump near by. The new location has ample parking space.

It is expected that the new area will be made ready during 1960 and be in operation for the winter of 1960-1961. About 1,000 feet of the slope has already been cleared of all the trees and rocks.

Benny Bernard, Oxford Store Room, is President of the club and Richard Giberson, Mobile Equipment Garage, is Vice President. Other Oxford men who are active in Chisholm Ski Club activities are: Leonide Arsenault, Thomas Grace, Jr., Melvin Poulin, Raymond Breau, Robert Roderick, Raymond Martineau — all Millwrights. Thomas **Arsenault and** Joseph Y. Arsenault of the Pipers. Reidar Christiansen and Wilson Gagnon of the Engineering Department. Raymond Hammane and Robert Fisher of the Electrical Repair Department. Raymond Roy, Finishing Department; Edward Libby, Salvage; Ernest Chennard, North Star Coater; George Elliott, Wood Department; John Roderick, Island Division; and James Peters, Meter Department. Active in the community are: Dr. Norman Jackson, Aurele Legere, Barbara Gagnon, Constance Roy, Wendell Broomhall, and Joseph West.

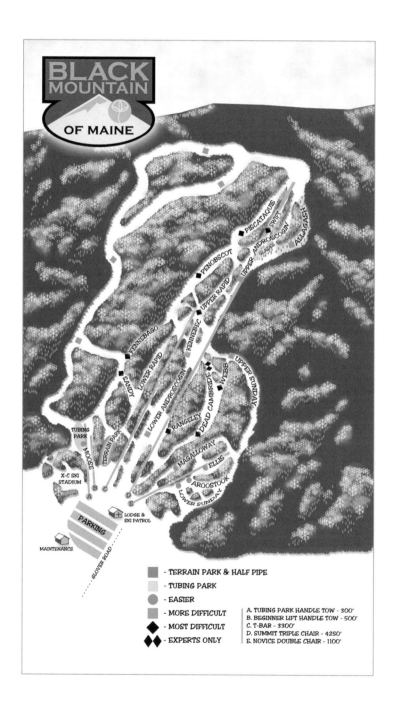

If possible, please make a donation
to our mountain:

Black Mountain Ski Resort
39 Glover Road
Rumford, Main 04276

Better yet, buy a pass and come ski!

❖   SkiBlackMountain.com   ❖

ABOUT THE AUTHOR

RICHARD KENT grew up in Rumford. He is a professor at the University of Maine and the author of 12 books. At Mountain Valley High School, he taught English, directed the writing center, and coached skiing, soccer, lacrosse, and track. With such coaching colleagues as Bill Morgan, Greg Waite, Ann Morton, Dave Morton, Jeff Turnbull, and Scott Broomhall, his ski teams won many conference titles and two *Class A State Championships*. His claim to fame as an athlete? Once, he roller skied the Indianapolis Motor Speedway track.

Skiing Indy, May 1978